Product of God's Mercy

BY

MRS. COMFORT AJALA (GRANDMA)

I0173558

First Edition
Copyright ©2024 Comfort Ajala

All rights reserved.
Published by The Lighthouse books, Agape Inc.

No part of this publication may be reproduced, stored in a retrieval system, or transmitted in any form or by any means, electronic, mechanical photocopying, recording or otherwise without written permission of the publisher.

Requests for permission should be addressed to the Lighthouse Books editor at editor@thelighthousebooks.com

Scripture quotations are from the New King James Version marked NKJV except otherwise stated. All rights reserved.

For more information regarding permission, write to:
The Lighthouse Books, 13721 E. Rice Pl, Aurora,
CO 80015.

ISBN: 978-1-950320-67-7 [Digital]
ISBN: 978-1-950320-64-6 [Paperback]
ISBN: 978-1-950320-66-0 [Hardback]

Visit us at:
www.thelighthousebooks.com
Printed in the USA

Dedication

To my Lord and Savior Jesus Christ, my King, my everything.
This book is also dedicated to the memory of my late
husband. To my children, you all are my joy and peace.

Contents

Acknowledgement

This book would not have been possible without the help of the Holy Spirit. All praise to the God, the Father of my Lord Jesus.

Special thanks to my children for encouraging me to realize my dream of writing my story. My God will bless you all in Jesus name.

I am grateful for the people of Kingdom Connection Christian Center, (KCCC), Denver, and Christ Resurrection Power Assembly, (CREPA), Jacksonville. You all continue to be bright part of my life. My God will continue to show you mercy.

My reserved thanks goes to Bishop Wale Oke for his constant prayers for me. God bless you, sir. To everyone who buys and read this book, I'm grateful!

Preface
(Testimonies from the Children)

My mother has a very strong spiritual background, and it was upon this background that she brought up all her children. To the glory of God, all my mother's biological children and their wives and husbands are in the ministry. My mother has never been a society or community centric woman. Most of her activities are centered on everything God. My mother is one who unites. Our mother was strengthened through the pains she passed through in life. Even during all those painful times, the grace of God carried her through. Her faith in God remains unquenched. Our mother has defiled several medical conditions even to the utter shock of medical consultants. When we lost our sister, Funke the first graduate of the family who rose to the position of director in Nigeria ministry setting, we thought that would have been the end of it for our mom. But by faith and grace, our mother survived this excruciating circumstance of losing a child, all by the grace of God. My mother is and has always been a cheerful giver. This has been my mother's gold standard. Thank you, mama.

– Pastor Dr. Emmanuel Ajala

Seeing grandma is seeing faith and grace in action. On numerous occasions, we would be with little or no food in the house, I remember that grandma would still take out of the little we had and give to men of God. Miraculously, someone will almost simultaneously, come to the house with money or food items for grandma and the family. Her generosity taught us faith and purpose. I don't remember seeing my mom sleep from the hours of 12 midnight till 3 in the morning. My mother is a praying woman, I'm so glad that I've inherited that spirit and passion of prayer from her. Grandma loves everyone that comes across her and she passed this attribute to all her children. We love you passionately grandma.

– Bishop Dr. Israel Ade-Ajala

My mother is a generous woman. I make bold to say that my mother is also a virtuous woman. She loves God so much that her entire being is God. She is a product of the grace of God. She is a very strong woman whose strength is renewed daily by the mercy of God. She is a woman of faith. She trusts God to always do the impossible for her. Her faith in Christ Jesus has never weaned nor weakened. Grandma has faced tough and rough times, but God has always show Himself strong on her behalf. Grandma, you are our rock!

– Revd. Dr. Omolara Idowu

My mom, as a trained teacher, is a disciplinarian, understandably so. She provided for us, she got involved in selling petty goods like banana, groundnut oil, and other minor retail goods to ensure that we were cared for. My mother is a woman of God indeed. She's very creative. When we were young, because we had no television in the house, she cut picture characters and shined torchlight into the box to create images for us to watch. I recall a time we had no food in the house, and mama asked us to pray. After praying, she asked us to search everywhere in the house for money. At the end of the search, we gathered so much money that was enough to buy food items for the house. My mother's prayer point has always been about other people and never about her needs and pains. My mom has a sincere and genuine love for God and People.

– Pastor Captain, Dr. Soji Ajala.

My mother is a godly woman. She taught us the love of God. She gave us godly foundation. She would always tell us that "whatever you want to do let God be the first." She would say, before eating prayer, before sleeping, before you make or take any decision, pray. If I'd to choose a mother, I would choose her a million times over. Her prayer life is worth emulating. What she taught us, is what we are teaching our children. Grandma is mother to all, who loves everyone. I pray for her that she will live more years to enjoy more of what she has worked for.

– Mrs. Eunice Awe

My mother! Grandma has always been a light that shines so bright to show us the way. I can say that mummy has always been good to us. She showed us the way of Christ. We went through difficult times, but mummy didn't give up on us or on life. She never takes anything about us for granted. We are praying to be like mummy. Mummy is good, she so nice a woman. Mummy is a person that forgives so easily. I asked her one day, "Why are you enduring this suffering?" Her reply was, "it is because of you, I don't want you to be alone here." She would in those days, all her salary to daddy. Her reason for doing that is because of the children. She created unity among the children. She would tell me, "Sola, you are the mother of them all…" I can talk about my mummy till eternity. I appreciate and honor her. Looking back, I'm so thankful to God that everything has turned to joy.

– Mrs. Olusola Adewole

CHAPTER ONE
The Early Years

Life is full of ups and downs. It is easy to dwell on and focus on the downs while we diminish and merely glance at the ups: that is the attitude of ungratefulness. Ungrateful person will be limited in greatness. Did you make the most of the ups and downs? Or did the ups and downs make the most of you? It is the road to self-pity when you dwell on the negatives of life. This is the trick of the enemy. The e has come to steal to kill and to destroy (John 10:10a) Don't allow the enemy to steal your joy.

I lived my life to the glory of God, I was raised to love the Lord, and trust His ways. Things that we see, feel or hear, and things we know sometimes could be contrary to what the Lord has in plan for our lives. I learned through experience that life was too precious to life by my senses. Early in my life I learned to put God first and to trust Him totally, is what matter most in life.

I was brought up to love God and love God's people. I was told a story of my childhood that made me develop the passion for prayer and positive declaration. The story was that I started walking late in life. I didn't start walking until I was three (3) years old. There was this uncle of mine who started calling me "the crawler." *Fidi wò,* is the literal translation in my mother's tongue.

Though I was a child, I had the clarity and boldness of mind to reject that name. God honored my little faith and confessions, and I started walking, thereafter. This experience made me develop a necessary spiritual muscle of faith, and to be outspoken when it comes to talking and declaring what God says about me, not what man says about me.

The easy things to do were to blame others, to question God or to just totally give up and accept what life gives you. I thank God that I was able to come to the realization early in life, that complaining, and blaming others will not bring me to my desired destination in life. You must partner with life to get the best out of life. Taking a back seat will put someone else in the driver seat on your journey of life.

My experiences in life, especially my early year made me who I am today. I was able to go out, make the money, buy groceries and still cook the meal – I was graced with the strength to be the person that I am.

I'm now aware that it was not my beating, spanking or disciplinarian prowess that made my children turn right, act right and live right. I, however, had to do the things that I needed to do to make sure that none of my children turn out bad. Wrapped by my tough exterior was a sincerely love and genuine concern for all my children. I was determined to do anything to make sure they all succeed in life. Think of this: you have a very difficult mother-in-law, you have a husband who was schooling abroad and not sending money back home for the family upkeep, you have seven growing children, you have your community people saying this and saying that what will you do if you were in my big shoes? Be as meek as a lamb? Or be as tough as a lion? Think of it!

I went to a Teacher Training College ran by a very respected institution called the Sudan Interior Mission (SIM). SIM shaped my life. This was where I became born-again, and my Christian life journey began and was nurtured. SIM was an international Christian organization. It was established in 1893 by its three founders, Walter Gowans, Rowland Bingham of Canada and Thomas Kent of the United States. Their goal was to share the gospel.

I was fortunate to be educated to the level where I could teach and train elementary school children. I was privileged to teach at an Islamic elementary school. The school became my mission field and my passion for the Muslim world was birth.

As an elementary school teacher, my goal was to raise great minds. I was determined to have children who will be great leaders and thinkers. I modelled great character, not only to my seven biological children, but to all my adopted children. To the glory of God, many of the children I taught are either great ministers of the gospel or leaders in private and public organizations.

As a young lady, I learned the act of farming. I was a farmer. I cultivated food items like maize, yam, cocoyam, plantain, banana, cassava and so on. I also retailed groundnut oil and palm oil. In those days, my backyard was filled with hens, fowls, goats, sheep, tomatoes, and vegetables.

Though I was active with farming, I was even more active in the work of God. The work of God has always been my primary focus. My involvement in anything that has to do with God is concerning not limited. As a child, my family attended the First Baptist Church, Oshogbo, I was also participated in the church activities of Christ Apostolic Church (CAC) and the Deeper Life Bible Fellowship, during their week for Bible study.

To me, it was God first. God before any other thing. I saw the secret of putting God first in the Book of Proverb chapter 3 verse 6. It says, "In everything you do, put God first, and he will direct you and crown your efforts with success." Today, I am so proud to say that I took all the right decisions by putting God first for He directed all my footsteps and crowned all my efforts with big success.

All the activities and experiences of my early years are centered on God, my Maker, my Creator, my Shield, and my Provider. The early years set the course for my entire life. It would be an injustice to the way I grew up, if I told you that it was all good, it would also be inaccurate if I told you that all was bad. It was the good, the bad and the ugly that paved the way for my today. Those early years held the touch to my present.

I remember a time when my children had no milk for their breakfast, but I heard a voice that told me to go and buy about six cans of milk and give to a priest. I obeyed this voice. I knew it was God that was talking to me. I had faith. I had patience. Faith that God will supply all my needs according to His riches in glory by Christ Jesus (Philippians 4:19, NKJV). Patience because faith and patience work and walk together.

I never complained or murmured. I did this because I knew it was what the Bible told us. In 1st Peter 4:9, NIV, the Bible says, "offer hospitality to one another without grumbling." I heard the voice of God and I obeyed without telling God that my children had no milk in the house for their breakfast.

Another miraculous story was the day when there was no food in the house. Yes. There was no food in the house. Remember, I had seven young, strong and growing children. I was a teacher in an elementary school. My husband was schooling in America. Also, remember that I was "mama generous." So, you can now see why there was no food in the house.

I called all my seven children to the living room. I told them there was no food in the house. I told them to pray to God to provide for us our daily bread. My children listened to me. They all prayed. After their prayer, I asked them to search everywhere in the house for money. They obeyed me again. And, they searched. At the end of this search, they ended up discovering money that was more than enough for our daily bread. Yes, they found surplus money that carried us for several days. And, I made pounded yam for them!

CHAPTER TWO

Secret of Raising Godly Children

I gave birth to seven biological children. They are the joy of my life. I would do anything just to see them smile. Raising them was not all the way easy. There were days that I didn't know what to do. The secret of my success when it comes to raising my children is an open secret – GOD!

The Lord helped me. Things worked out well, though, many times I had no idea what I was doing. The mistakes I made in parenting, the Lord turned it around, and they became testimonies. I surrendered everything to God with reckless abandonment. God raised the children He gave me. God knew that I had no power of my own. He knew that He was all and all for me. God saw my heart. God saw how much I believed in Him.

I put my absolute trust in God. God's word became my guide. The Lord became my all in all. I was a disciplinarian. With all my strictness in raising my children, I sincerely could not say that it is the beating, or the yelling that made my children to turn out great. I In raising godly children, I needed the help of the Lord more than anything. Raising my children while my husband was not around was very challenging. I had to be the father and the mother. It was difficult to play both roles at the same time.

Raising children should not just be about what you tell them to do or not to do. What they see you do counts too. I made sure that my children saw me pray, read my bible and go to church. The summary of my experience in raising godly children was that showing them was a more effective strategy than telling them. Don't be a parent that says, be a parent that do. Model what you want your children to be.

It is important to train your children to have the fear of God, and the fear of home. Don't let *good morning* be missing in the mouth of your children. Say good morning in your house. Train your children to say "hello". You may think this is simple, but it will help them in life. Teach them to say, "good morning" "good afternoon", "good evening". Don't let it be your children that walk pass people without acknowledging them.

I thought that there was no manual that you could read to help you raise godly children. I was wrong. I discovered the life manual called the Bible – the Word of God. It was the manual for raising godly children. I raised my children the way I knew best. I knew I didn't do everything right, but I did whatever I saw in the Word of God.

I believed in the scripture that says, "he who spares the rod hates his son." (Proverbs 13:14, Majority Standard Bible). I believed in the scripture that says, that, "the rod and reproof give wisdom, but a child left to himself brings shame to his mother." (Proverb 29:15, ESV). I believed in the scripture that says, "train up a child in the way he should go; even when he is old, he will not depart from it." (Proverbs 22:6, ESV).

I prayed for my children, and I prayed with my children. I disciplined my children, and I didn't spare the rod where whooping is necessary. I didn't do everything right, but the Lord helped me. I will admit that it was not being tough on my children, *I had to*, and *"beating"* them that shaped their lives. It's the Lord that showed me mercy. The scripture in Isaiah 54:13 (ESV) was fulfilled in the lives of my children. Thus, "all your children shall be taught by the Lord, and great shall be the peace of your children."

It was God's mercy. It was God's grace. It was God's favor that helped me. I'm not claiming to be the most perfect parent, but I turned out to be the perfect parent for my children. I made sure that my children prayed, read their Bible, and heard the Word of God all the time. Part of raising my children are the many testimonies that they have seen. Those uncountable testimonies built their trust muscles in the Lord. On several occasions, we had nothing to eat in the house. So many times, we went to bed without food – we just drank water and went to sleep. There were many days and nights that the Lord provided for us miraculously.

One of such nights that stood out for me was when we had nothing to eat, I asked my children to pray to God to provide food for us. Innocently, the children prayed. After praying, I told them to go search around the house for anything they could find. At the end of their search, they found enough money to make a meal that night. Only God's mercy did it!

On another occasion, after a prayer of trust to the Lord that night when we had nothing to eat, God used someone who saw one of my children and blessed him with enough money to make dinner. Truly speaking, it was the multiple miracles of God's faithfulness in our lives which my children experienced first-hand that shaped their lives.

CHAPTER THREE
My Ministry

I have a ministry of prayer, which I still passionately enjoy.

Growing up, there was a believe that the power of darkness and that of the witches gathered at midnight to destroy people's destiny. With that knowledge, I made up my mind that I will operate in the spirit realm in prayers during that same hour to pray for my children (biological, spiritual, adopted). I started this practice years ago. It became a common practice in our house. When my children went to bed, I was up praying.

Let me leave this word of advice to parents: please model the habit of praying to your children. Don't just tell them to pray, let them see you pray. They will follow your example faster than your advice!

Reading God's Word helped me to pray. I have always been a lover of God's Word, and that has helped me in my prayer life. I encourage everyone to fall in love with the Word of God and to also make sure that their children fall in love with the Word of God early in life.

I introduced all my children to the Word of God early in life. Reading, studying and memorizing the Word of God was very important to us as we developed the lifestyle of prayer. This lifestyle of prayer won't come easy, but with commitment, dedication and consistency, you will start growing in your prayer life and start enjoying the hour of prayers.

Years ago, shortly after my husband passed, there was an event that happened. Around midnight, on a certain night, we started hearing weird noises outside, in our compound. My children and I started praying in our living room that night. We started declaring the judgment of the Lord upon the works of Satan. We called the sword of the Lord to cut into pieces all the agents of darkness. The following morning, we saw dead and dismembered cats inside our compound. We didn't understand how that happened. However, I believed that it was a great deliverance of God that day.

I have seen the Lord answer prayers in mysterious way. Sometime the answer to our prayers came immediately. Other times, the answers came suddenly. Yet, many other times, it took a while for the answers to come. But one thing I knew, was that the Lord answered our prayers – and He is still answering our prayers.

In my ministry of prayer, I noticed that there was power in the sent word. I understood by experience that you could pray for someone in another part of the world and that person would feel the impact of your prayer and the Lord will do what you requested. I got many testimonies from people whom I stood in gap for, and they received their answers – answers have come in form of healing, deliverance, open doors and provisions, among many others.

I knew from the beginning of my Christian faith that Interceding for people was a powerful tool. In my prayer ministry, I prayed for those I knew and those that I didn't know. I urge you to pray for others, whether they are far or near. This one secret you must know: praying for others, even when you have your own needs, is very powerful. I grew up praying for other people. Asking God to provide for them even when I didn't have enough to provide for my children. Every time, without fail, God, will pour out His blessings by meeting our needs.

Get a prayer partner. I had a prayer partner whom I prayed with every week. With a prayer partner, you will be accountable to one another. Being accountable and having an accountability partner is a good way of life. If you want to go fast, they say, go alone, but if you want to go far, go with others. Live by this good word in your prayer life. I encourage everyone to have prayer partners. Even Jesus asked His disciples to join Him in prayer on His way to the cross. Join force with a trusted partner in prayer.

One of my beloved prayer scriptures was one of the shortest verses in the bible, "Pray without ceasing." (1 Thessalonians 5:17, ESV) I took that literarily. Instead of engaging in idle talk, I just developed the habit of talking to God. I really loved talking to God because it made me happy and gave me so much joy. There was no need talking to people who couldn't do anything about my situation. I just talk to God Who is the only One that would do something about my situation. I remembered this clearly.

I needed no one to encourage me to pray. I'd seen prayer turn things around for me and for the people that I've prayed for. I remembered when I was back in Nigeria, I declared it by faith that I will live the latter part of my life in the United States of America, and I had no idea how it would happen. The Lord honored that prayer. I also prayed that all my children would know and serve God. The Lord honored that prayer also. Don't tell me that prayer doesn't work. I know it works.

The Bible remains the best and only place you can go to if you don't know how to pray and what to pray for. You can draw near to God when you pray. You can hear Him when you pray. I remain a living testimony of this. I prayed, and prayed, and prayed, and still praying and the Lord answered and is still answering me.

In all these, the journey of my ministry was a very deliberate one. It was very intentional. Intentional because I purposefully decided, with the Holy Spirit guiding me, to live a life in service to God and love for humanity.

I was sold out to the will of God. Serving God was the only desirable option to me. My children followed on the same path, and this started with Tunde, my first son. Tunde led the other children by modeling good example, and by introducing Christ to them, as they all followed.

I followed the leading of the Holy Spirit. I did not follow what my culture wanted me to do. It is good to have an ear for God when He speaks. I thank God for making me to hear Him whenever He spoke to me.

CHAPTER FOUR

MANY TRIBULATIONS

"Do everything without complaining and arguing, so that no one can criticize you. Live clean, innocent lives as children of God, shining like bright lights in a world full of crooked and perverse people. Hold firmly to the word of life; then, on the day of Christ's return, I will be proud that I did not run the race in vain and that my work was not useless. But I will rejoice even if I lose my life, pouring it out like a liquid offering to God, just like your faithful service is an offering to God. And I want all of you to share that joy. Yes, you should rejoice, and I will share your joy." (Philippians 2:14-19, NLT).

The word of God urges us to live a life free of complaining and grumbling. I saw all my pain as gain!

In everything that appeared as a pain, I saw a lifting from it. I got strengthened and strengthened after each battle God made me win. I have seen my own share of troubles. I have seen troubled sea – I either walked on water or the water parted. I have faced mountains – I was either given the strength to climb the mountain or the mountain moved. I had found myself in the fire at times and in the lion's den other times – I came out unscratched and un-scourged. I don't look like what I have been through, all to the glory of God.

I fought battles that physical weapons could not deter. I fought wars that the opponents were invisible. The Lord fought for me against those wicked agents that came to ask me if I saw what they sent to harm me. The Lord defended me against the evil agents that sought my life.

I didn't need to fight in the battle. All I did was to hand everything over to the Lord, the One I serve. The battle is not yours but God's (2nd Chronicles 20:15; 1st Samuel 17:47, AMPC).

I am sharing some of my challenges to inspire someone to hold on to God no matter what. If you are going through any difficult times, you will be through. When the sorrow of life multiplies yet the Lord remained good, His faithfulness was sure. "Though the fig tree may not blossom, nor fruit be on the vines; though the labor of the olive may fail, and the fields yield no food; though the flock may be cut off from the fold, and there be no herd in the stalls – yet I will rejoice in the Lord, I will joy in the God of my salvation." (Habakkuk 3:17-18, NKJV).

I have seen the Lord's goodness, God's mercies, God's compassion; the Lord has been so good to me. Any pain I have seen, or experienced in my life cannot be compared to the good I have seen in these my years. In the late 1960s, I got so sick that I was in coma for about three months. No one knew if I would come out of that sickness and challenging times alive. I knew that God got me. The last words to my children before I was incapacitated for months was, "this will not kill me." It was a dark period and uncertain times. I had no idea what my tomorrow held but I had absolute confidence in the One who holds me in the palm of His hands.

On another occasion, in the 1980s, I was not given any chance to live. I was diagnosed with a cancerous-like ailment. My children were told to take me back home from the Teaching Hospital and provide me with palliative treatments to make end of life easy and bearable. I was given months to live. While I was home, a foreign object came out of my ear, by itself. That was the end of that. Almost forty years after the end-of-life diagnosis, I can testify that where medicine failed, and medical professional gave up on me, my God stepped in and did the needed surgery to save my life. The same chief medical officer at the University Teaching Hospital, who gave me months to live, said with his own mouth that "Someone has gone in, and neatly done the surgery." According to science, I should be dead and buried in the 1980s. This is the same me that I am writing a book in 2024.

Part of the pain of life that I endured was that loss of one of my children in 2012, my daughter, *Funmilola*. it was a very difficult time for me and the family. I grieved and sorrowed, but I never questioned God – not because I was a superwoman, but because I know whom I believed. I have had pain, yet I have had joy unspeakable. My life is a testimony of what God can do with a life of someone who totally trust in Him.

CHAPTER FIVE

Before I Leave

Let me announce to you that the entirety of my life has been all about God's abundant mercy to me. God has been too merciful to me. I was written off by people, but God counted me in. I have been called foolish for seeking the face of the Lord, but God called me His chosen for serving Him. I have been called a drunk, but God knows that I was simply pouring out my soul before Him. Many wanted me to put my trust in them, but I chose to put all my trust in God.

God's mercy has always been sufficient for me.

I've had near-death experiences, but God's mercy restored my life. Doctors had pronounced my bones as wearing off speedily, but God's mercy had strengthen my bones.

CHAPTER SIX

Secret of Living Long

God said, "with long life I will satisfy him." (Psalm 91:16, NKJV).

Also, in the Book of Ephesians chapter 6 verses 1-3 (NIV), the Bible said this: "Children, obey your parents in the Lord, for this is right. "Honor your father and mother" (this is the first commandment with a promise), "that it may go well with you and that you may live long in the land."

There are so many places in the Bible where God gave us instructions on what to do to have long life.

In 1st Kings 3:14 (ESV), the Bible said, "And if you will walk in my ways, keeping my statutes and my commandments, as your father David walked, then I will lengthen your days."

The Word of God has been my secret. If you live by the Word of God, day and night and believe in it, you will live long. The Book of John said that "And everyone who lives and believes in me shall never die. Do you believe this?"

If you keep God's commandments, you will live long. The Bible told us in Proverbs 3: 1-2 (KJV), "My son, forget not my law; but let thine heart keep my commandments, for length of days, and long life, and peace, shall they add to thee."

When I read in the Bible that I will not die but I will live to recount the deeds of the Lord (Psalm 118: 17, International Standard Version), I claimed it immediately. I did not think twice. I began to sing it as my song every day of my life. It was in my mouth every day and every time. I believed it. Yes, I believed this verse in the Bible that said that I shall not die but live.

You may ask why I believed in this verse of the Bible that said that I shall not die but live long. I saw, in the same verse, that all I had to do to live was to confess what God has done for me in my life. When I started to remember all the good things God has done for me, I had no other choice than to praise Him all the time.

I honored my father and my mother. No argument about this commandment. When you honor them, you will be blessed with long life. (Exodus 20:12, KJV).

Very importantly, when I found out this secret of long life that God promised us, I did not play with it. I did not only honor my father and mother, but I honored everyone that was called God's servant. Their denomination did not matter.

I obeyed my parents. I honored them. I respected them. I did what they asked me to do. I did not do what they didn't want me to do. I truly honored them. Honor your father and mother so you can live a long life.

Honoring everyone and everywhere is good virtue. It will not take anything out of who you are. Rather, it will add long life to you.

1st Peter 5:5 (ESV) says, "Likewise, you who are younger, be subject to the elders. Clothe yourselves, all of you, with humility toward one another, for "God opposes the proud but gives grace to the humble."

It pays to be humble. Humility is good.

Remember, also, that in Genesis 6:3 (NKJV), that God promised that we live up to 120 years. So, if God has promised us this, it should not be surprising that I am still here today. I am here today because I know that God is not man that He should lie. God's Word is yes and amen.

I have faith in God's promises of long life.

All my life, I put God first. By putting God first, you are putting the Word of God first. By putting the Word of God first, you are reading it every day and every night, and it does not depart from your mouth.

Do all these, and you see how God will satisfy you with long life just like He promised.

I will continue to pray for you as you read my journey of God's mercy. The God that answered my prayers will not leave you. He will not forsake you. He will not abandon you. The mercy of God will be all around you. God's mercy, grace and favor will make a way for you where there's no way. You will increase in God's power. You will eat of the goodness of the land. You will inherit the hidden treasures of the land all the days of your life. Your children, their children and their children after them shall be called blessed. I call you blessed!

Blessed be the Father of our Lord and savior Jesus!

www.ingramcontent.com/pod-product-compliance
Lightning Source LLC
Chambersburg PA
CBHW070753050426
42449CB00010B/2449